PETALS FALL

By the same author:

A Common Garment

PETALS FALL

ANITA PATEL

RECENT
WORK
PRESS

Petals Fall
Recent Work Press
Canberra, Australia

Copyright © Anita Patel, 2022

ISBN: 9780645180893 (paperback)

 A catalogue record for this
book is available from the
National Library of Australia

Cover image: © Anita Patel, 2021
Cover design: Recent Work Press
Set by Recent Work Press

recentworkpress.com

For Scott, and our family

In memory of Yvonne Valerie Patel (nee Stanley)
1931–2018

Contents

Vanished

My wedding dress disappeared
mysteriously—to my mother's
consternation…
so many hours had gone into
this frothy concoction
of Italian lace and pale pink ribbon
(reminiscent of handmade
party frocks from my childhood)
She had folded it carefully into
a Chinese camphor wood chest
(owned by her mother)
smoothing gossamer
billows into submission
pressing them gently
into the comfortable
darkness of ancient wood—
but one day when she
peeked into the dimness
it was gone…
all of the creamy, flower
embossed sweetness
vanished…
like flimsy dreams
for a cherished daughter
who did not share her sorrow
at this loss—but gratefully
received the empty, teak hard
box carved with galloping
horses, swaying trees and
boatmen crossing a stormy river.

Tempting Providence

My grandmother pressed a black thumbprint
on my forehead whenever anyone called me a pretty baby
Don't tempt Providence, she said—*it doesn't do to plan or praise—*
who knows if someone's listening (spite is all around us)
She lit candles, hung St. Christopher on a golden chain
around my neck, prayed for our souls—sifting rosary beads
through her dainty fingers, reminded Providence daily of her dread...
So when you proclaim our happiness with certainty—
my heart quakes at your buoyant voice—I touch wood,
I taste the sour metal of St. Christopher in my dry mouth,
the press of a blackened thumb on my forehead.

Sungai Besi, 1941: War Begins

Ah Peng bundles us off the verandah—dragging us from toys, snacks and the shady branches of a rambutan tree. The makeshift air raid shelter stands in an unused mining pool. Tiny translucent shrimp somersault in pale ripples. Before I know it, my feet sink into wet sand. My hands dip and flutter in cool water.

Ah Peng is shouting: *Nei soeng sei maa? Do you want to die?* She hauls me out and plonks me on a wooden bench.

The bright sky booms and shatters. Our world dissolves—toys, snacks, rambutan tree, shady verandah, rippled water, sunshine...

I am quiet on the hard bench, in my closed fist a wriggling shrimp.

My daughter looks like your daughter...

(Rita's story)

When the officer with a samurai sword arrives, my older sisters scuttle into hiding. They know the fate of pretty Eurasian girls in time of war. We, small ones, gather around my mother as she answers the door.

The officer speaks to her in English: *In my country, a mother with many children is honoured.*

Then he looks at me—a skinny eight year old, fringe pasted flat over my black eyes. He pulls a photo out of his wallet. *My daughter—looks like your daughter.*

And there she is—my Japanese twin. Her straight hair chopped into a bowl, her dark eyes gazing at me. Her father tucks her back into his pocket.

The next day tins
of food appear at our door.

Sister Harriet

Sister Harriet, the Japanese nun,
sits on a tiny stool outside the convent latrine
squat as a small toad, pock-marked
and uncoiffed (she is an Asian nun after all
and only deserving of a bonnet)
All day long she tears paper so skipping,
strutting girls can wipe arses.
Girls who piss on the floor as soon as
she mops up the mess, whose laughter
stains the baleful air outside her cell.
Poor Sister Harriet with her thick tongue
unable to pronounce words in Malay
or French or English, teased by monkeys,
tormented by girls, bullied by a pink-faced
Mother Superior—poor Sister Harriet
swishing her broom and grumbling, grumbling
until the day soldiers bash on the convent door—
small men from the country of her birth—
suddenly Sister Harriet is promoted from
toilet to parlour, and the staccato stiffness
of her syllables holds the enemy at bay.

There were coconuts...

When my whole world ended
I learned to husk a coconut
for there were no more dinners
from fine china on the rosewood
table—but there were coconuts
angled neatly on the ground,
rapped sharp and deft with a mallet,
segment after segment of fibrous
outer skin removed
and the hard roundness struck
(with the blunt edge of a *parang*)
it's all in the precision of that tap—
spilling sour water from two perfect cups—
and then the careful grating of each
half shell on a *parut*
the snowy flesh falling soft and sweet
into the tin plate of my new life...

Travelling to Tampin

On the train to Tampin with our luggage safely stowed, I gaze out
at jungle and plantations, monkeys in green branches, coconut
trees, *kampung* houses. The Malay couple across the aisle is sharing
nasi bungkus and *kerupuk*. I am cheered by their laughter and the
chugging tug of station names: Batu Gajah, Kampar, Tapah Road,
Tanjung Malim, Rawang, Sungai Buloh, KL Sentral, Bandar Tasik
Selatan, Kajang, Seremban—trips to Kajang for *satay*, the Hakka
mee in that Seremban rest house, my grandmother's home in KL…

One year later I find your journal:
It was a very long drive from Kuala Lumpur to Tampin in Negeri Sembilan.
After days of frantic planning, we were fleeing to a rubber plantation in the jungle.
The day was exceptionally hot and muggy. I sat uncomfortably between my two sisters.
When we turned off the road into the jungle, it was much cooler. The car jolted along
a dirt track into a fringe of vine tangled trees. We were filled with sadness and terror…

I wish I could have thought of you as I travelled to Tampin on that fast train, inhaling
wafts of *nasi bungkus* and admiring the view…

The sticky smell of fear inside the black Austin, your parents' hushed voices,
your sisters' tears, the hectic escape into unknown darkness.

queda de pétalas: fragments of a Eurasian childhood

soft as *kebaya* lace,
               fragrant as *kayu manis*,
                            sweet as pineapple tarts
      jingli nona, jingli nona   twilight thrum
and twang
yo kereh kazah—singing voices, dancing feet—
               find Nanny's rosary beads, girl,
                     fetch the sirih box
tea and cake with *atas* cousins—
                        itchy-poky party frocks
           twirling *branyo*—drenched in holy water,
      spiked with *sambal blachan,*
dark as *kecap* on boiled rice,
                    funny as uncle's *sarong*
               dropping
sting of *rotan* on backsides   aunty's slipper flying
clatter of mahjong tiles
                    guitars
                strumming
      hantu everywhere—
                      a
                  saint for any
                  occasion
        so many people at the table
eat some more—*makan lah, makan lagi*…
              amor minya amor, amor minya
              korasang

queda

        de

pétalas   all those

           petals

              falling

       falling

            falling

A drawer full of saints

My blind aunt had a drawer full of saints—
St. Joseph, St. Theresa, both Francis Xavier and
the one from Assisi, St. Bernadette, St. Anthony,
St. Christopher (dozens of heavenly denizens
on frail prayer cards) jostling in the scent of
eau de cologne and Tiger Balm, tangled
in ebony rosary beads and sprinkled
with holy water from Lourdes…
Her favourite, by far, was St. Jude (the patron saint
of lost causes) even though he had never come
close to answering her prayers…
My aunt played the piano in a life before her eyes failed,
she enjoyed films and babies and making ice cream—
and maybe she loved someone more than life itself
but (as the saints know) a sightless, simple woman
has no right to dream and no stories to tell.

Three Candles

(from my mother's memories of her mother)

My mother lights three candles on the altar. One
for Jesus, one for Mary and one to ward off evil spirits…
The nuns tell us that it is a mortal sin to believe in
witchcraft and demons. We should only fear Satan.
My mother goes to church each Sunday, kneels to say her
rosary, prays a novena, wears a scapular but she knows
that it's not Satan who creeps through the tall grass, lurks
in leafy branches or bangs a window shut. This menace is
far closer to home—*hantu, jembalang, pontianak,*
orang minyak, pocong, pelesit, toyol, mata jahat—
vampire ghost and goblin child, blind flap of owl or bat,
oily man, grasshopper sprite, shrouded woman, and that
ever present malicious eye watching small children at play…
My mother drives a nail into the trunk of the mango
tree, she heeds the warning chirrup of a gecko, she boils
milk till it flows over the pan's edge, she places crumbs of earth
in the mouths of her children, she is careful not to waste
a grain of rice, she bows her head to the guardian
of the door. She lights three candles on the altar.

Pantun

(A pantun is like a hawk with a chicken; it takes its time about striking – Malay Proverb)

Today, I hear about pantoum
from real poets who write sonnets
and sestinas, who know about cinquains
and tercets and tricky meter…
and I think of *pantun*—that ancient
pattern of four lines—two couplets
(*sampiran dan maksud*) hanging
together like dew drops on a silken thread—
hovering between shadow and purpose—
gaib—palpable and inexplicable—
Four lines recited by courting couples,
sage grandparents, cheeky cousins,
witty friends—bandied about playfully
or declaimed sternly as a lesson or a warning…
Today, I hear about pantoum from real
poets who display their flawless interlocked
quatrains ("in a form adapted by the French
from Malay folk literature")
I think of *pantun*…

Kampong Chicken

Supermarket chicken not same like kampong chicken
no taste lah—kampong chicken got muscle because run
around—very delicious—the meat brown colour—
this supermarket chicken so soft, so white…
as white as mansions standing in neat rows
where women once swept sandy paths
and children whooped and chickens scurried—
small joyful birds—scratching in red earth—
vivid squawk of lively feathers chased and cherished,
slaughtered lovingly and eaten with relish.

The Minor Third

I have no ear for music
but I sing songs I learnt from you
when I was too small to talk—
And when a poet from another land
points out the minor third (that
hop and twang of three sassy semitones—
reminiscent and familiar)
I hear it everywhere—in sirens and
bird calls and my grandchildren's voices,
I hear it again as I enter hawker stalls
in Tiong Bahru where we ate our
favourite food together
(when I was too small to talk but not
to sing) I hear it tapped out
on a cheap keyboard:
Someday I'll wish upon a star
and wake up where the clouds are far behind me
tears in chicken rice,
the salty broth of your voice…

Come to the Manger

Come, come, come to the manger, children come to the children's king
Sing, sing chorus of angels, morning star over Bethlehem sing...

(Traditional Christmas carol)

I am not the Virgin Mary, milky white, veiled in blue,
that role belongs to Margaret with the golden hair.
I am one of the children who come to the manger,
kohl eyes shining in my small brown face, dressed in
a *lengha* and *choli* cut from my mother's oldest sari,
my friend Lorraine steps beside me wrapped in vibrant
Jamaican colours. *Cheongsam, sarong, kaftan* and *kurta*
parade, brightly, on the lit stage. Our parents cheer as
we deliver gifts to the Christ Child. Margaret with the golden
hair smiles sweetly, as we kneel in front of the Virgin Mary.

Vengeance

I left my baby outside a sweetshop—
tucked up neatly in her pram, fast asleep.
When I came out, my baby had gone. Nothing
in the pram but a bit of old blanket. The loss
was too much to bear. My mother promised
to buy a new baby but I was inconsolable until
the sweetshop lady said, *Them wicked kiddies*
who stole your dolly will get nothing but black coal
and hard rocks from Father Christmas.

She knew (that woman in a flowered overall,
scooping magic out of glass jars all day) that
a few drops of sugared vengeance in a bag
of lemon sherbets was the best remedy
for a five-year-old broken heart.

Port Alma (1971)

If it was today, we would have
taken a photo of ourselves
and posted it on Facebook
maybe even videoed
each other gazing at the view:
sharp peaks of white
knifing the stark sky—nothing else
except sun worn grass and dry wind—
What would we have looked
like in that photo?
my father, wearing a new shirt,
pointing out the astonishing salt
hills of Port Alma (our last stop
before Sydney)…
my mother's glamorous sunglasses
hiding the trepidation in her eyes…
Would the picture have disclosed
our bewilderment at the lack of trees or homes
or people? or would we have been
caught in a tidy pose—the immigrant
family—mother, father, twelve year old girl,
her little sister and a very small boy
seeing their new country
for the first time?

Cocky's Joy

Hidden under precious papers,
your citizenship certificate,
a pretty document (almost half a century old)
ornamented with sprigs of wattle and
our national fauna (kangaroo and emu)
bearing the coat of arms...
You loved wattle and kangaroos
but your heart cracked, just a little, on the day
that you received this award...
After the ceremony we ate damper spread
with golden syrup: *Cocky's Joy,* someone said—
words that held no meaning for a woman
who preferred rice to bread, but it was a party
(of sorts) so you smiled and watched your children
devour a stranger's food—knowing that in the evening
you would nourish them properly.

Storm

He'll need this, the kind nurse says
placing a white chair neatly
in a corner of the shower cubicle
and as she adjusts the nozzle
to a tepid drizzle, I see the rain
crashing in heavy dollops out of
a tropical sky on you—leaping under
sheets of water in a pair of 1960s
bathing trunks, brandishing a bar
of yellow soap—hair glistening,
skin drenched, teeth as white
as the chair that sits in this new bathroom—
the rain tumbling on your laughing
face and on our skipping feet
as the sky rips open above us
spilling the rush and call of a storm
that we thought would last forever...

Blemished

I peel stickers off pears and oranges,
remembering your irritation at labels on fruit—
we come from a place of *durian* and *duku*,
from *nangka* and *manggis* and *rambutan*
cut ripe from laden branches…
You would enjoy (I think) the bowl
of blemished apples on my kitchen bench—
pitted and scarred—from a friend's
crooked tree—not red enough
or green enough to earn a fancy sticker.

Ice Cream

(for Dad)

Your thin fingers scoop
the last dribble of melting white
from a paper cup—
not pistachio gelato or raspberry ripple or
knickerbocker glory with a flourish of
both our spoons over the tall glass,
just a vestige of vanilla wiped
from your dry lips—
and I weep for a pot of sugared milk
bubbling on the fire,
a kitchen perfumed with cardamom
and saffron, nuts chopped and piled
on a board, your big hands stirring,
stirring until the turn of milk to cream…
and all of us waiting
for a cone of *kulfi*—bright as sunshine,
fragrant as an Indian bazaar.

Picking up the post

(from family letters to my mother as a student in England 1951-1955 found after her death)

After your jewellery has been spilled
and sorted—gold bangles counted carefully
and divided by three—rings chosen and claimed—
and all the pearls distributed…
I find myself in the dusty back bedroom—alone—
floundering in a rustle of voices tipped and tumbled
on the floor…
>   *fat aunty makan*
>   *all the curry puffs at teatime,*
>   *Lyn's charm bracelet (dropped*

somewhere
>   *on the way to Mass),*   *Uncle Eric*
>   *back from*
>   *the jungle with a wild piglet (alamak!)*
>   *squealing and*
>   *running all over the kitchen…*

Dolly's first baby (safely delivered),
>   *cousin Ernie (so naughty lah) fired his catapult*
at a hornet's nest … got stung on the nose,
>   *Mummy playing*
>   *mahjong twice a week*
>   *Joy's Confirmation shoes—very expensive (white patent*
>   *leather),*
eat well, stay warm,
>   *come back,*
>   *come home…*

Here I am, in a crumpled clamour of faded ink—
and there you are, in winter darkness, taking off your overcoat,
slotting a shilling in the gas meter, picking up the post…

Ready for Sale

Ready for sale—polished to a fine sheen—
every room tricked out to charm a buyer—
not a trace left of old Malacca or Bali or
India or Spain, your paintings lifted
from the walls, all the vintage *Penguins* gone
with the Chinese altar table and my grandmother's
carved dining chairs...
Ready for sale—squeezed dry of laughter and tears,
angry voices, wild arguments, love and fear,
food cooked and relished, family gathered and dispersed—
the sweet and bitter juice of all that life scooped out
                                             and flung away...
Ready for sale—swept clean of dust and story...

         but in the front garden—green fragrance
         rustles in branches of the curry tree
               planted on that first day.

Cracked

My grandmother's mixing bowl cracked
on the first day of lockdown. I mended it as best
I could, but I knew that it would never again
endure a robust beating with mixer or wooden spoon.
I mourned this tough old vessel freighted from
England to the Far East nearly a century ago
and transported to the Antipodes to live in a
home now also gone—today it sits in my kitchen
cupboard filled with lesser bowls. I will use it to
crumble butter into flour with my cool hands or maybe
to soak dried fruit in French brandy at Christmas time—
I will wash it in warm soapy water, rinse it with care,
and gently towel the ragged hardness of its scar.

Parchin kari—The Tiler

In our suburban garden—a man
slices stone as neatly as a piece of cake.
Standing in a plume of dust and noise
he flips and frosts the oblong tile
with just enough mortar—notching three
perfect stripes in one deft stroke—
I think of carnelian, agate and garnet,
turquoise, sapphire, malachite, jade
crafted on a metal wheel—four centuries
ago (when circular saws were just a dream)
and illusion became reality on the banks
of the Yamuna river…
In our garden—the tiler surveys his handiwork
then two muted thuds with a soft mallet
and the smooth hardness set in place
as flawlessly as lapis lazuli in white marble.

Bhakti (Radha to Krishna)

Sit gentle while I twine your hair
into a silken plait, ornament your
brow with a scarlet teardrop, slip golden
bangles on your wrists and fold my
sari soft over your blueness...
now you place your peacock crown
upon my head, wind your saffron dhoti around
my milky thighs and I sigh with the pleasure
of it all ... I lift your flute up to my lips
and beckon you to follow and you follow
me with your eyes downcast, my earrings
glinting in your lobes, I reach for your hand,
my hand ... you hear my heart, your heart...

Rangoli

Each morning a woman makes art
at the entrance of her house—
lotus petals and mango leaves
spill from her fingers…
flowers blossom on the ground,
fish swim, peacocks strut
on a welcome mat for Lakshmi—
and when the goddess has stepped
inside and ants have eaten their fill,
the mat is swept away (every tiny
grain blown free)
Her broom swishes washed earth
tomorrow she will make art again…

Alakshmi (Not Lakshmi)

I started life as Lakshmi—golden skinned, dressed in pink,
delicate as a lotus, pulling gilded rain from the sky—
they marvelled at my shining face, put sweets into my rosy mouth
and bathed me in milk, but it was far too good to last...
my lotus brightness shrivelled, my skin darkened,
a crow tugged at my footsteps and sweetmeats turned
sour as dried limes ... they wept at the sight of me—
a shrunken, owlish creature bespectacled and bookish—
but what a relief to put an end to all that capricious abundance...
I knew that Lakshmi was as fickle as moonlight in a puddle
here and gone—in a shower of glittering
raindrops which was always going to leave us wet and cold...

You will take the flowers...

Your long winded explanation of *om* fills my mouth with yawns.
Your voice goes on and on, and to keep myself from blinking I reach
out to the dancing shimmer of my peacock.
Your anger blackens the air, and I am condemned to wander the
courtyards and pavilions of this temple as a shabby peahen with
downcast eyes. There is a strange joy in this peaceful temple life but I
know that you will return when you have cooled down.
You will take the flowers from my beak and turn me back into
Parvati, your wife, but when will you lose your temper again?

Red Thread

Trapped in a staff meeting
as a Principal in fancy shoes
holds forth—I suddenly think of the
red thread that bound me to a chair
in my first classroom...
the teacher wound it round me
quite gently (but with purpose)
I couldn't really blame her—
I was a wanderer and not one
for learning (unless the lesson
contained a vivid tale and this woman
was hardly going to tell the kind of
story that thrilled my childish heart)
I was held in place by scarlet thread
but my feet tapped out a beat
under the wooden desk...
I watch the Principal's coral lips
squirming like a pair of glistening
slugs—maybe they will wriggle
off her frazzled face...
the power point presentation
bursts into a spurt of slimy bubbles—
the Principal squeals in empowered
excitement—I finger the red thread
at my waist, my feet tap out a beat...

Yukata

After dinner in Miyajima I dare
to visit the *onsen* on the bottom floor
of our boutique hotel…
Two women show me how to use stool
and shower to clean myself
in all the secret places that women
know so well…
I slide into bliss of heat and forgetfulness…
somewhere in the distance
soft voices patter over my melting skin…
Afterwards I wash quickly and (suddenly
aware of my nakedness)
I scramble on my *yukata* like a sloppy
dressing gown—eager to be gone
The women tut tut as I come out
into the lit dressing room…
Gently but firmly they remove
the untidy garment (dove grey sprinkled
with pink and white peonies)—they
fold the *yukata* deftly—
left side over right—across my breasts
then reknot the dark purple *obi*—firm
around my waist—their pale hands
move like familiar friends adjusting
the soft cloth—pulling it this
way and that—till I am wrapped
in a field of flowers and all our faces shine.

Rosewater Women

The Hindi word *dalit* can be translated as
divided, split, broken, scattered...
like a handful of rose petals flung into
sugared water to flavour *gulab jamun*
soft, delectable, melt in the mouth
dumplings...
but there is nothing soft or sweet
about the furious jangle of a
thousand bare feet pounding the
earth as a rose pink army
advances—undivided—
ready to break and split
and scatter—
brandishing *lathis* like swords,
seeking retribution with bamboo
sticks—shaming the cruel husband,
the rapist, the murderer, the thief,
the wife beater, the bully—
(unafraid to thrash a culprit black
and blue)
bringing the *gulabi* fragrance
(of whole and perfect roses)
into unsugared lives.

Women's Wellness

(Bev's story)

My nana's house is now a wellness centre
for women, she would have loved that—my nana
who was never allowed to be unwell because
it was washing day or baking day, and the children
needed to be fed, and the vegetables had to be
scraped and boiled to make the stew go far...
How she would have loved the idea of wellness
for women—my nana, who never mentioned
the pain that came at night sliding over
her chest like a brown snake waiting to strike—
women's wellness would have made her sing,
(the mind-boggling madness of such a thing)

Metamorphosis

(in memory of Maria Sibylla Merian 1647-1717)

It is not natural for a young girl
to gaze at insects night after
night—painting moments of
startling metamorphosis
till the candle sputters into
a waxy stub and pages gleam with
unknown light: the slow
weaving of a silken pod, wet wings
shaken out of gauzy husk,
seed pearl eggs on green leaf
and all those caterpillars
disappearing without a trace...
surely it is sorcery—these proofs
in jewelled paint of stunning
transmutation—when so many
clever men still believe that frogs hop
out of raindrops—your accounts
will not be well received...

they will pin your thorax to a board
and leach the colour from your wings
and classify you neatly:
woman artist
prone to flights of fancy...

but it's time now, Maria,
to release you from the shadow box
of scientific scorn...

unfurl your hidden wings and fly—
    all your colours blazing—across a shining sky.

What Are Your Sins?

Walking to confession
Bless us Father
two by two in checked pinafores
and straw hats—glad to escape
out of the classroom into the sunshine…
just a short stroll to where you are waiting
to forgive us…
For we have sinned
mocking Sister Mary Immaculata's
bum wobble and lying to our mothers
and smoking in the toilets and swigging
from a stolen bottle of Blackberry Nip…
We have sinned: flaunting
our scarlet lips and boob tubes
and glittery toenails and hot pants…
We have sinned hopping into panel vans,
hitching up our sports tunics and unbuttoning
our blouses to lure boys…
These are our sins…
But what are your sins dear Father—
sitting behind the shuttered
window in that dark cupboard
listening to our girlish misdemeanours,
mumbling benedictions
and handing out Hail Marys like bitter pills
to cure us of our badness?
What are your sins?
Have you confessed them?
And can they be instantly forgotten
walking back to school on a sunny Tuesday?

The Final Cut

Washing dishes in that first kitchen,
(gazing at a garden waiting to happen)
wiping the sticky bloom of jammy
fingers from walls and doors,
unpegging sun-warmed clouds
in the creaking breeze,
shelling peas for dinner, patching knees,
reading another story, singing another song,
filling the nappy bucket one more time
before the baby wakes and cries...
every frame of this film tinted tender as
a dream—hours of tiredness and tedium
edited out of the final cut.

Nerine lilies

Nerine lilies bloom in April—
a gift for me as I swell and
slow, waiting and waiting
in that first small house, reading
my way into other lives, dreaming
of places I have never seen,
while in my own garden—
hot pinkness pushes its way out
                 of wet earth

In Shukkei-en Garden (Hiroshima)

We wander through a shrunken world
patterned lovingly by Ueda for Asano—
sound of water, all the seasons,
Mountain of Peace and Blessings,
Pond of Cleansing Purity, Koko Bridge
(straddling heaven and earth)
and deep within the soil
under yellow irises and green herbs,
pine trees and peonies,
under White Dragon Stream and
Cool Breeze Tea House and
Field of Good Harvest—
so many crumbled bones
fallen forever on that day when
willows and cherry trees blazed
in the place where friends used to rest.

Past the Torii Gate

Did he come from Miyajima—
that young soldier with the round face
peering through my grandmother's
store room window? *Jack in the Box*,
she called him because of his inclination
to pop up when least expected
with offerings of food for the baby.
Did his father own this soya sauce
shop, now humming with tourists
jostling over ceramic jars of miso paste?
Did he walk these sandy paths to the
Itsukushima shrine and watch boats
sail past the *torii* gate?
Did he gather oysters as big as his hand,
feed the wild deer, and carry his own baby
up the slopes of Mt. Misen?
Does an old man somewhere on this
pretty island recall his round faced
father, dressed for war, sailing away
past the *torii* gate to an unknown land?

Genbaku Dome

Birds fly through the skeleton
of Genbaku dome—
skimming blue curves
between steel ribs—
high above our tilted faces
birds fly—
swooping through gaps
in the bones of Letzel's
masterpiece—
flitting and floating over
rubble covered ashes

Snapshot

*("Little Children on a Bicycle" mural
—George Town, Penang)*

At the right moment
the cat walks past (a slim ginger
tom on flicker light paws)
the children go on pedalling
on the peeling wall unaware of
all that tourist clamour…
the cat slips down an alleyway
just after the camera clicks
and catches him forever—an
insouciant slink of gold fur—
padding past Tan Yi and Tan Kern…

Goa Gajah

It was only a matter of time, Ganesha,
before they flicked on that artificial sunshine
and left you sitting in a pool of yellow
dazzle—blinking your eyes in
fluorescent glare, for these beams
strike needle sharp
        after centuries
                of cave darkened solace.

Butterflies and Bodhisattvas

No flowers at the top of Borobodur,
no earth for trees to grow
yet butterflies shimmer
among faces fixed in silent meditation—
up here where sightless eyes
regard the changing landscape
century after century—
vivid scraps of life skim blithely
over headless Buddhas and
stories told in crumbling stone.

Dulang

On the edge of a rice field,
stitched in impossible green,
a woman rinses *dulang* tenderly—
setting out row upon row of washed gold
waiting to be burdened with gratitude
for the flourishing green, the coconuts
and tiny chickens, for the little boy
flying his kite, for the white kite soaring
like a bird, for crimson ginger flowers
and the sky, and the tapping of hammer
on wood, and the green…

Moment

In this stolen summer of cinder and
smoulder and blaze and ash...
I watch a woman pull a fish from the
ocean—foil flashing flutter against
the evening sky—a shiny fish flag
unlatched quickly and flicked
into rush of sea on sand...
I see the silver of it disappear gratefully
beneath the cool swell...
Fish and sea and sky and woman
and my smoke heavy heart salved
(for a moment) in this stolen summer...

Wollumbin

Wollumbin—Cloud Catcher—
holding the whole soft sky in your
                              warrior arms
Your face tip tilted to the sun,
rainbow tinted, lightning struck,
starlit, swathed in thunder, etched
clear against morning…
                    long before *warning* was a word
                              in a faraway language.

Almost Spring (2020)

Outside my window magpies
squabble over bark and twine
(their music curdling drizzled air
this dull damp morning)
they wrestle for best bits to
build their nests—unaware
that everything has changed
since they tapped their way out of
last year's eggs...
For magpies—it is almost spring
time to tug choice morsels from
wet earth, tussle over twigs and worms,
make new homes and sing...

in my pocket this morning…

snowy crumbs of shattered
shell, soft sand and a small hole
just big enough for one of your fingers
to poke through (but definitely getting bigger)
my windcheater sags with the memory of
damp gifts crammed into its fleecy pouch:
mermaids' scales, coral charms, pearly
rainbow coins and gemstones scooped
from pools of treasure—your footprints
small and smaller raced back and forth
along the glossy shore, the salty sky
redolent with voices of children and gulls…
and this morning—in my pocket

a small hole

Waraburra and Wattle

How the waraburra presses its passionate purple
purpose against the wattle's golden blaze—
whispering darkly into all that yellowness...
How it twines its pea-petalled tendrils through fragrant
inflorescence, twisting and turning in the downy sweetness
of those steady arms...
and the acacia bending slightly—yields her bright branches
to the ardent knot and tangle of this demanding wanderer...

Molonglo Water
(Jerrabomberra Wetlands)

It's not the ocean that holds my heart
though I have walked at its unending edge…
It's not the clamour of waterfalls—that muscular
tumble of cascading white though I have
bathed in pools of emerald light…

It's simply … a glimpse of reed and ripple—
shadow mottled glimmer beneath a Canberra sky—
colour of earth and leaf water—filled with frog song
and webbed feet—swoop of beak and wing water
spilling into billabong, swamp and creek—
been there forever water—stories to tell water—
Molonglo water … washing
        every corner of my dusty heart…

Unfastened

Sometimes we need to leave
the poem behind...
and wander among shelves of soft yarn—
sea blue and grass green, burnt gold
as autumn leaves, yellow as lemon peel,
all the tints of a pigeon's neck—
it's good to take home a bag of light
and shadow—to hold skeins of twilight,
rose and lilac—make tea and sit
with a friend (or alone), unfastened
from the mystery of our own hands as
needles and hook turn thread
to cloth.

Notes

'Sungai Besi December 1941: War Begins': This poem is based on an extract from my mother's journals.

'Sister Harriet': This poem is based on an extract from my mother's journals.

'There were coconuts…': This poem is based on an extract from my mother's journals.

'Travelling to Tampin': In 1942 the Japanese army entered Kuala Lumpur, the capital of Malaya. My grandparents left the city and took their family into hiding.

In 2019, I caught the train to Tampin on my way to Malacca. A year later I found my mother's journal and discovered that her family had escaped to a rubber estate in the jungle in Tampin, Negeri Sembilan.

'queda de pétalas: fragments of a Eurasian childhood': This poem is a tribute to my Eurasian (Kristang) heritage and is inspired by the *peneira poroso* poetic form which was developed in Kristang communities descended from Portuguese and Asian marriages in the 18th and 19th centuries. The *peneira poroso* is also known as *queda de pétalas* (petals fall).

In the *peneira poroso*, fragments of no longer than seven words are spread across a page with uneven spacing. The placement of words is said to be shaped by the aesthetic "breaths" of the poet. (https://formsofsea. blogspot.com/2017/04/the-peneira-poroso-poetic-form)

The Portuguese / Kristang lyrics in the poem are from the popular folk song, *Jingli Nona*, which is accompanied by the Portuguese communal dance the *branyo.*

'Pantun': Pantun is an ancient form of Malay poetry. It is regarded as high art and is an integral part of classical Malay literature. It also thrived as a natural part of daily communication in traditional Malay society. (Wikipedia)

The pantun is made up of two opposing couplets. The Indonesian critic, Gazali, writes that the link between these couplets is mysterious (*gaib*) yet palpable to Malays and Indonesians. After reading the first couplet one feels an expectant vibration of the message which is to come via the second couplet. (Gazali)

'Parchin kari—The Tiler': *Parchin kari* is a Persian word for the ancient technique of using cut and fitted polished gemstones to create inlaid images on marble. Its most lavish expression is found in the Taj Mahal.

'Bhakti (Radha to Krishna)': The relationship between Lord Krishna and his divine consort, Radha, represents *bhakti*—which means love, devotion and worship in Sanskrit. The clothing exchange between the two symbolises their shared essence and pure devotion towards each other.

'Rangoli': Every morning in India, millions of women draw intricate patterns—called *rangoli*—in rice flour on the ground in front of their houses. *Rangoli* are an invitation to welcome Lakshmi, the goddess of prosperity, into the home. Rice flour is used to provide food for small creatures like ants and birds. Through the day, the drawings get walked on, washed out by rain or swept away.

'Alakshmi (Not Lakshmi)': Lakshmi is the beautiful goddess of wealth, luxury, fortune and power. She is also called Chanchala, the one who is whimsical and always restless. Alakshmi, the older sister of Lakshmi, is the goddess of misfortune and discord. She is ugly with a shrivelled body, dark skin and beady eyes. She is associated with the crow and the owl.

'You will take the flowers…': When Parvati, Shiva's wife, got bored by her husband's tedious explanation of the mantra *Om Namah Shivaya*, Shiva turned her into a peahen and condemned her to live in Kapaleeshwarar temple. After many years of repentance and prayer, the peahen finally found Shiva and offered him flowers that she carried in her beak. Shiva then appeared to Parvati and reunited with her.

'Rosewater Women': The Gulabi (Pink) Gang is a group of Indian women activists who fight discrimination and violence against women. Members of the group wear pink saris and wield sticks. The group originated in Banda district, Uttar Pradesh. This district has a large Dalit (Untouchable) population. Dalit women are at the bottom of both caste and gender hierarchies.

'Metamorphosis': This poem is based on the largely untold story of Maria Sibylla Merian (1647-1717) a pioneering naturalist whose meticulous observations conclusively linked caterpillars to butterflies, at a time when women were still being burned as witches and when being a curious, intelligent woman was very hazardous indeed. The fact that Merian was an artist who had no formal scientific training (because women at that time were barred from university education) also played a role in the efforts of male scientists to discredit her. (Reference: Tanya Latty, 'Hidden women of history: Maria Sybilla Merian, 17th-century entomologist and scientific adventurer', *The Conversation*, 21 February 2019).

'The Final Cut': *He was a filmmaker who evoked, unlike almost anyone else, the dream life that… is at odds with the very prosaic way that our lives actually play out. We seem to remember our lives a little bit like poems or dreams and yet we live them very absorbed by prosaic details.* (Jason Di Rosso, ABC Radio National, on the films of Federico Fellini)

'In Shukkei-en Garden (Hiroshima)': Asano Nagaakira (the *daimyō* of Hiroshima) began construction of Shukkei-en Garden in 1620. The task of creating the garden was given to the tea master Ueda Soko. Shukkei-en means "shrink-scenery" garden. When the atomic bomb was dropped on 6 August, 1945, people sought shelter in the garden. Many of them perished.

'Past the Torii Gate': The torii gate is usually found at the entrance of a Shinto shrine and symbolically marks the border between the ordinary and the sacred. One of the most famous examples of this gate is at the Itsukushima shrine in Miyajima.

During the Japanese occupation of Malaya, a young soldier frequently visited my grandmother's home bringing gifts of food for her baby. He told her about his little son left behind in Japan. I visited Miyajima in 2019 and wondered if this island could have been his home.

'Snapshot': *Little Children on a Bicycle* mural in George Town, Penang is based on a sister, Tan Yi and her brother, Tan Kern.

'Goa Gajah': Goa Gajah (Elephant Cave) Temple in Bali dates back to around the 10th century. There is a small alcove with a statue of Ganesha inside the cave.

'Dulang': *Dulang* is the Balinese word for a special tray used by women to carry tall offerings *(gebogan)* of fruit and flowers to temple ceremonies.

'Waraburra and Wattle': *Waraburra* is the Aboriginal name for *Hardenbergia violacea* also known as *Happy Wanderer.* It derives from the Dharug and D'harawal languages of the Wa'ran (Sydney) region.

'Wollumbin': The mountain Wollumbin is a sacred place for people of the Bundjalung Nation. Legend has it that thunder and lightning are caused by battles between warrior spirits of the mountain, and the facial profile of a warrior chief is in the mountain outline. Wollumbin means cloud catcher or weather maker.

In 1770 Captain Cook gave Wollumbin the name Mount Warning. It was a landmark to 'warn' English mariners of the treacherous coastline.

Acknowledgements

My warmest thanks to Shane Strange for taking another chance on me, and guiding me through the process of publishing my second collection. I am so grateful for his skill as an editor and his kindness as a friend.

Thanks also to Moya Pacey, Sandra Renew and Jen Webb (lovely poet friends) for their wisdom, humour and generosity.

I would like to acknowledge: my Eurasian cousins who can talk for hours about our extended family; Rita Nash and Bev Fenwick for sharing their stories; and Padma Menon who has connected me with the archetypes of my Indian heritage and shown me the goddesses.

Thank you to Mum who scribbled in journals and hoarded letters and to Dad for his memories.

And thank you with all my heart to my husband, Scott, and our children (Anil, Asha and Tarla) for their unending love and support.

Many thanks to the editors of the following publications where some of these poems (or versions of them) first appeared: *Not Very Quiet*, *The Blue Nib Literary Magazine*, *FemAsia Magazine*, *Cicerone Journal*, *Backstory Journal*, *Other Terrain Journal*, *Plumwood Mountain*, *Burrow*, *The Canberra Times* and the anthology, *This Gift This Poem* (Puncher and Wattman).

About the Author

Anita Patel's collection of poetry, *A Common Garment* (Recent Work Press) was published in 2019. Her work also appears in publications such as: *Cordite Poetry Review, Mascara Literary Review, Cha: An Asian Literary Journal, Backstory Journal, Other Terrain Journal, The Blue Nib, Not Very Quiet, Plumwood Mountain, Eucalypt: a tanka journal* and *The Canberra Times*. Her poems are included in the anthologies: *What We Carry* (Recent Work Press), *Australian Poetry Anthology* Vol. 8 2020 and *This Gift, This Poem* (Puncher and Wattman).

Her poem 'Women's Talk' won the ACT Writers Centre Poetry Prize in 2004 and her poetry was selected for and published in *Australian Book Review's* States of Poetry ACT, 2018.

She has performed her work at the National Folk Festival, Poetry on the Move Festival, Queensland Poetry Festival, at Smith's Alternative and at Word in Hand, Glebe.

www.ingramcontent.com/pod-product-compliance
Ingram Content Group Australia Pty Ltd
76 Discovery Rd, Dandenong South VIC 3175, AU
AUHW020721050325
407891AU00005B/32